LAD'S LOVE

SYLVIA KANTARIS
Lad's Love

BLOODAXE BOOKS

Copyright © Sylvia Kantaris 1993

ISBN: 1 85224 194 2

First published 1993 by
Bloodaxe Books Ltd,
P.O. Box 1SN,
Newcastle upon Tyne NE99 1SN.

Bloodaxe Books Ltd acknowledges
the financial assistance of Northern Arts.

LEGAL NOTICE
All rights reserved. No part of this book may be
reproduced, stored in a retrieval system, or
transmitted in any form, or by any means, electronic,
mechanical, photocopying, recording or otherwise,
without prior written permission from Bloodaxe Books Ltd.

Requests to publish work from this book
must be sent to Bloodaxe Books Ltd.

Sylvia Kantaris has asserted her right under
Section 77 of the Copyright, Designs and Patents Act 1988
to be identified as the author of this work.

Cover printing by J. Thomson Colour Printers Ltd, Glasgow.

Printed in Great Britain by
Cromwell Press, Broughton Gifford, Melksham, Wiltshire.

*Old Man, or Lad's-love, – in the name there's nothing
To one that knows not Lad's-love...*
     FROM 'Old Man' by Edward Thomas

Acknowledgements

Acknowledgements are due to the editors of the following publications in which some of these poems first appeared: *Aestus, Edge* (Japan), *The Observer, Outposts Poetry Quarterly, Phoenix* (Australia), *Poetry Review, Printed Matter* (Japan), *Stand* and *World's Edge* (USA/Japan).

Lad's Love was completed with the help of a major Arts Council Literature Award in 1991.

The author photograph on the cover is by Daryl Kibblewhite.

Contents

9 Hybrid
10 An Old Story
11 Early Warnings
12 'Let him kiss me with the kisses of his mouth'
13 Love Talk
14 Since you ask
15 Earthworks
16 Animals
17 Jane Fonda, your mother, and me
18 Sky-writing
19 Air-Sea Rescue
20 If there's time
21 Charmer
22 Future Prospects
23 Intimations
24 Hair-line Crack
25 To Her Sleepy Lover
26 Before You?
27 Night Watch
28 Fruits
29 Toy Boy
30 'When you are old...'
31 No I'll never
32 What Lasts?
33 Letting Go
34 Be missing you
35 Post partum
36 Disappearing Act
37 In Absentia
38 Old Haunt
39 Finds
40 Jammed Brakes
41 On Westminster Bridge
42 Words
43 Between Us
44 A Change in the Weather, Underground
45 Last Remains
46 Last Year in Dorset
47 The Proposition

48	Washing Instructions
49	'For Refund, Insert Baby Here'
50	Writing for Two
51	Cold Shower
52	Cross Words
53	Happy Ever After
54	Explication de Texte
55	Something Like a Wedding?
56	The Ring and Gobbledegook
57	'Home'
58	'Domestic'
59	£50 Compensation
62	*Other books by Sylvia Kantaris*
64	*Biographical note*

Hybrid

I bruise more easily than in my youth
and you knew that, planting your fingers
in my arm where the flesh is softest.
Did you mean it as a floral tribute
to what might have been if I were young enough?
The bloom's exotic but a dead-end hybrid.

What else could germinate out of a cross
between your future and my past except
this sad memento mori I call
Orchis-Hermodactylus and watch
its inky purples fading even as I write
about the silly dream I had of Lad's-love?

An Old Story

'Young Apollo,' I call you, winningly.
You smile and turn and offer me
your profile, a cameo.
Tracing your outline now with a light touch,
to be sure you feel it,
I wonder how it is that you with your fine
shining hair have grown
entangled in my shadow.
I think you must be half in love with death.
You ask if I am jealous,
folding me so tightly in your arms
I can't breathe.
Surfacing, I tell you I am very greedy
and jealous of my great-great-granddaughters
parading their white hips into eternity.

Early Warnings

1

We've looked us up in Dictionaries
of Classical Mythology, in Robert Graves
and hundreds of encyclopaedias.
We don't exist, except in tragedies.
Leander drowned and Hero killed herself;
Sappho's lost lad lies in jigsaw pieces;
Phaedra and Hippolytus won't fit now that
historians insist the two were of an age
(and anyway, we're sick to death of suicides).
I'm no Jocasta, you're no Oedipus.
Why should we need to look for precedents
amongst the wayward ancients, just as if
time hadn't changed the way things were once?
Yes, sod the lot! Let's go to bed instead.

2

Did the earth move? Did you feel the house quake
when the bombers throbbed low over the roof?
It's a thrill a minute living near an airbase!
Well then, back to precedents. This book says
Helen couldn't have existed in the flesh
since she'd have been too old for Paris to have loved,
according to historians. When Troy fell
it wasn't for some middle-aged old slag.
(Menelaus comes without a date-tag.)
You can tell that these authorities were shocked
by the anomaly (their word) but fixed the facts.
So the town came tumbling down due to a mirage
of an ageless female face? What chance for us
against a whole sky charged with patriarchal business?

'Let him kiss me with the kisses of his mouth'

Dreaming I'm awake again, I dream
in your arms. *Behold, thou art fair, my love;
behold, thou art fair.* What has not been said
already in The Song of Songs about your attributes?
Thou art beautiful, O my love.
Perhaps your twin balls haven't quite been
dwelt upon enough. (I dwell on them,
and would compose a hymn to your silken scrotum.)
Lacking a language to do justice to your phallus,
I tease it tenderly with tongue and teeth.
You are all perfect in all parts, beloved –
hair, eyebrows, fingers, lips; even your biceps.
Let me groove over your bearded youth,
your mouth on mine, the way our hands clasp
like sea-creatures copulating suck to suck.
I am all grovelling worship of your crevices.
How incomparable are thy feet!
You smile. Kiss me again while you're still dreaming
we shall never wake. How shall I guard your sleep?

Love Talk

You told your mother, so I told my son.
'To be rid of that Jocasta crap', I said.
But as we lay together between sky and sea,
half-sheltered from the wind by marram grass,
the myth still lay between us, didn't it?
That's why I closed your eyelids, crooned
words – how a playful, radioactive breeze
could snuff us out in no time. (Politics?)

Your answer: 'Just so long as we both go
at once, like this', was what I wanted
as you closed in and your face grew featureless.
Such deaths we live, invoking even
an ill wind to lay the ghosts of myths
that should be long out of season – to rest.

Since you ask

What others? (I'm forgetful, simply want
to blot *you* out now, blot us both out in
one flash of black light, to finish it
and keep you in the nowhere of a moment's
stopped breath.) You are the last. Enough.
I can only hear your heart-beat and
the muffled breakers with my eyelids shut
against your coming. (Why were you so late?)
Release me, fold me closer, suffocate.
No 'other lover' has so dried my mouth
with such anticipation – except one,
your age exactly and your simulacrum,
who was lost at sea for all time
nine months before your birth.

Earthworks

I keep thinking of his fingers which are
far too subtle for such work, though he insists
that digging up old graves appeals.
'Just exploring,' he whispered the other night,
excavating with such expertise, you'd have thought
I might dissolve. They needed someone with experience
as a temporary hand (Youth Opportunity indeed!)

He said he'd had a lot of practice at the job.
(What did he mean by that?) We mix a musty scent
between us, which won't wash off.
Is his talk of finding couples with their
finger-joints entangled just a form of foreplay
(dabbling in a timewarp of perspectives)?

'Most bones we find are spongy, some melt
instantly, you're scared to breathe.' I held
my breath until I nearly suffocated and
he sealed my mouth with his as if to kiss
me back to life while thrusting deeper
and my body felt like earth.

I wonder what remains he came across?
Some Iron Age pelvis (female), clumps of thighbone,
a tangle of old hair like rusty hemp?
I'd settled, I'd told him, I was not prepared
to be exposed to such a vulnerable afterlife,
and drew the sheet up, but he drew it back,
defined my ribcage delicately with one fingertip.

Animals

Something fishy going on next-door-but-one,
and she's no chicken. Mutton dressed as lamb,
the missus says. Must be cuckoo if she thinks
we can't see through the privet. Some young stud
(can't be more than thirty) strutting up the path
like a tom as if he owned her old man's place,
though she keeps it like a pigsty, that's a fact.
You should hear some of the noises they make.
Once, the wife heard her yelping, thought she might
need help, but we didn't interfere, just in case...
well, what with what you read in the papers –
and I can tell you both our doors are double-bolted –
he could have had a twelve-bore up his jeans,
on top of which we think she might be dangerous
(been to Green-and-Common, my old woman says).
I bet the bugger's sizing up what he can pinch.
That property must be worth a bit. The bitch
is begging for it when you come to think.
Bloody Welfare State keeps *him* in rut,
milking the taxpayers. It gets my goat,
working like a donkey to support subversives,
at it every day like fucking rabbits. ('Scuse my French!)
The cow even protested against Neighbourhood Watch.

Oh love! As if the world were watching us!
As if each of our meetings were a TV summit!
What am I scared of? Hold me closer, tight.

Jane Fonda, your mother, and me

It wasn't out of fear of your mother
that I wouldn't meet her. On my own I'd dare,
since she said over the phone she didn't care
about my age, just wanted you out of *her* hair.
It was the memory of the jeans I used to wear
before they shrank on me that was the matter.
You said you'd have them but had given them to her
I noticed when I saw them on the chair
by her bed that afternoon when we lay there
(nothing Freudian, you said, just comfier)
and I cast your mother in the image of Jane Fonda.
So since I couldn't equal *her* now, either –
same vintage as myself but shapelier, leaner –
how could I let you see all three together?

Sky-writing

Three days away from you; four still to kill.
The vapour-trails of Phantoms are heading westward
and will reach you before this letter does.
The plush hills here quiver like a stage-set
but I cling to any crazy link between us
even if it ends with a full-stop.

This afternoon I strolled along the bank
the river carved so long ago it doesn't
matter. Anyway, the landscape is as changing
as the water which has not dried up yet.
A Harrier thundered past, I stuck my fingers
in my ears and watched a clod of mud collapse
and dissolve like the gap between us as we tread
the same earth, not expecting it to last.

Air-Sea Rescue

And so you think of anything but us
when we're together, do you
('the wind rasping the mainstay,
some ship far out at sea...'),
your mind tacking even as you crest me?
Such absence in our presences!
I wasn't with you either in the act.

Today my mind was on those helicopters
combing the coastline. For vessels in distress?
(They call it 'air-sea rescue exercises'.)
It seemed to me as if we were washed up
and I was spying out a mirage of us
mouth-to-mouth amongst the marram grass,
each having failed to bring the other back.

If there's time

If I outlive your passion; if there's time;
if there's time for me to shrivel while
you're still as young and lithe as I still feel,
I'll grow as wild and cracked as Piere Vidal,
'the fool *par excellence* of all Provence',
and cackle his refrains in a doss-house.

Hot is such love and silent.

Who'll guess that I was ever once that she-wolf
of the song our bodies understand like absence
in advance? My words come back at me like echoes
from another time and place but I can almost
hear the voices in the chamber of your mouth –

God curse the years that turn such women grey!

And if I'm Crazy Jane at last, still
croaking old tunes when you've journeyed out of touch;
if we have time to slip this splendid madness,
my song will say you crossed my path at least,
and I shall laugh if there is time, love;
if there's time for anything on earth.

Charmer

I watch you charm the woman in the bread-shop
who will serve you first despite the queue. I'm jealous.
How you use your winning smile! I hate
the way you switch the blue-eyed-boy look on
unless for me alone – and even then, what
I love best are all your other faces, passing
frowns and knots. More than that, I love to wash
your smile off with your sweat and mine until
we both grow faceless, bodiless, in close-up,
our veins so interlaced we can't tell which
of us is which. (Whose arms are these? Whose legs?)
The Carmagnole of love is merciless.
Your private face is nowhere, blots the light out,
as the woman in the bread-shop might have guessed.
I love the way that my smile haunts your lips.

Future Prospects

I guess the uniforms have too few hours off
judging by the way the missile-carriers
unzip the clouds and flash their underbellies.

There was a hymn that could have been 'Ancient'
or 'Modern' when I learnt it, but it's bang on target:
Live each day as if 'twere thy last.

Aren't we lucky to be living at this moment
when the heavens are opening and years don't count
any more than radioactive cardboard-cutout sheep?

Basking naked as whales under the greenhouse effect,
with Nimrods for mood-music, what on earth else could we ask
beyond the prospect of an endless future sealed in permafrost?

Intimations

As bereft as a child lost in a supermarket,
I snivelled *sotto voce* like a grown-up.
One minute you were there and then you weren't
and then I was an alien on a planet
inhabited by giant ants with shopping-bags.
They knew where they were going with such purpose,
interweaving back and forth and forth and back
as in a ritual dance I had never learnt the steps of
and never would again in your absence.
It's hard to explain why I bawled so much,
so loudly, when you reappeared, but children
do that too when they regain their anchorage
which, if they'd never had they'd never miss.

Hair-line Crack

This last winter when we sat out on the lawn
the cruel sun undid your youth a bit
by highlighting a single silver thread
amongst the golden. (I bleach all mine out.)
You'll have more soon and I'll be glad of it
since when you're sixty and I'm eighty-odd
(supposing not a single hair-line crack
irradiates us first) we won't seem ill-assorted.

Youth ages quickest; I can wait while you catch up.
We may both be bald for months before we're dead.
Midwinter heatwaves have the heartening effect
of drawing us closer and a hair-line crack
or two will cancel all our differences
so you'll no longer need to drop my hand in public.

To Her Sleepy Lover

But at my back, those giant New Zealand lizards
on TV, remember, love? Imagine living
four hundred years in such slow motion!
Can you calculate how long it would take
to copulate at that rate? And say that coitus
were interrupted by his need to sleep
just as she was nudging up to climax?
She'd have a long time to adore each part,
as I've been doing, right up to your eyelids,
for years it seems. And did my lazy tongue
interrupt your rest for no good reason –
mere speculations about lizards in rut
and whether they are up to it for months
on end, or just flick on and off?

Before You?

Well, there was only one whose back is still
disappearing round the same corner
thirty years ago now. How should I know
how many faces I've grown through and out of since?
A few stay fixed, in photographs. I think,
'I loved him-only once, or thought I did'
but can't feel how it felt. It's like
trying to remember hunger after a feast.

This time it's different, it's real. I know it
by the emptiness I feel in your absence;
the way you won't yet shrink into a photograph;
by my fear of blind spots, disappearances
round corners – and above all our connivance
in the act of growing faceless to each other next.

Night Watch

'I thought you'd died, and I was scared to death.
You just stopped breathing for what seemed like ages.'
Perhaps you dreamt it or perhaps I did,
but I remember that, throughout the night,
at frequent intervals you thumped my back,
quite gently but enough to jump-start my heart,
just in case, although you don't remember that.
You didn't want me dying in your sleep.

It was a comfort to me. I relaxed
into the measure of your beat like a foetus
lulled by sea-thuds as in amniotic waters,
utterly secured by the lifeline between us,
but by morning you were upside down in bed.
You didn't want me dying in your birth?

Fruits

I'm sick of guilt. Was it my fault that
the Burma Star Association had positioned
their most pitiably maimed to rattle tins
outside the supermarket? We pretended
not to notice, kept our hands in our pockets,
engrossed in our first-ever argument,
which would have been our last if I had not decided
I was old enough to carry all the blame, like
a worn-out shopping-bag. (You have your youth to thank.)
But that was afterwards. Meanwhile, I was thinking
as I shopped that most men of my own generation
had been brainwashed by military service
in peacetime. Coming home on leave, intact,
they took possession of young girls with courtesies
like roses from a shop, played escorts, played hell
when I footed my own bill in restaurants.

And now you dare to scorn the Women's Movement?
I'm trying to 'take over', make you 'servile'?
Listen, love, although I got no medals, I've been
bunged into a ditch, manhandled, sat on, kicked,
had my glasses ground to smithereens by boots.
I'm a veteran of protests (Aldermaston,
Suez, Vietnam, Greenham). It was never fun
trying to protect an earth for you to live on.
That supermarket sickened me, it was so stuffed
with profits from skin, sweat and rags – and what
exotic names the fruits have! But you just hate shopping
and that's all there is to it, whereas I could have wept
over Outspan oranges, sun-ripened with Soweto's dead.
I stared at the rich produce of the Nato Pact, cursed
the weapons manufacturers. Like you I would have
simply preferred to be bored to death instead.

Toy Boy

*Men now outnumber women in the 16-35 age group
by 212,000. The toy boy phenomenon could make sense.*
 THE OBSERVER

Why don't you try one? Mine's a lot of fun.
I turn the key and wind him up. He whirrs.
His clockwork heart ticks very, very fast,
as fast as mine, almost. Alas, the mechanism
of my own's so rusty, I expect the strain
of this new spring is bound to crack it up.

(An out-of-date model, madam; breakages
should be expected when antiques are fitted
with new parts. You're lucky yours has stood the pace
so long. It's not worth anything of course,
unless its sentimental value to yourself.)

Meanwhile my toy boy plucks the rubber bands
that keep my head hooked to my neck and the rest.
(I disassembled all my dolls; the worst
kept saying 'Mama' till I cut the crap
with scissors. All of them were sexless
except celluloid Kewpies which announced the Barbie Age.)

Last night I tried to take my new toy boy to bits,
thinking he might be an Action Man in camouflage,
but he said he couldn't cope with a Kalashnikov.
'O brave new world!' I tried to say, but gagged
when he told me he'd have to cut my head off
if I couldn't keep my trap shut and stop winding him up.

'When you are old...'

So you'll take care of me when I'm past it
(propped on a commode)? Oh I believe that,
can already see me nodding by the fireside,
you kneeling at my feet, or bending down
to rub my aching back with liniment –
if you can still bend since years level us
in time if there is time enough or not.
Our love will grow as passionate as grass
if there is still grass... I'm forgetting
where I was. A pilgrim soul or something?
My mind wanders through the future of our past.
But I do believe you mean it for the moment
while we still walk in step, your trainers
and my scuffed gypsy sandals pacing the dust.

No I'll never

No I'll never leave you, it's still
as I said and meant that day in Zennor,
and we bypassed the Men-an-Tol
because we couldn't wait to get back here
to bed instead of wriggling through the hole
of the birthstone. We'd done that before.

No I'll never leave you – it's forever
as I said and meant in Speedwell Cavern
in a wet boat on an underground river
ferried by a muscular young Charon.
I fancied we could even outlive life together
holding hands tightly, I was so far gone.

No I'll never leave you while I breathe
as I said and meant daily, nightly, everywhere
we travelled. 'Even after death'
I whispered to myself, for good measure.
The first death happened on the prom in Weymouth
when your hand dropped and left me with a stranger.

No I'll never leave you if I can discover
which grave is ours before the names wash off.
I'm no longer deceived by this other
who has taken over. Once we used to laugh
even at blank stones in the churchyard, remember?
But that was way back in our second month.

What Lasts?

Of course it won't 'last' since we're both alive
and everything living must rot. The roses
you picked for me, so choosily, are dead –
except one yellow one I hadn't noticed
(not quite surprising; it was still a bud).
Today I was surprised by it. Overnight
it had opened up. 'Fool's gold,' I thought.
Why still expect the unexpected?

You'd placed that bud amongst the rest on purpose
so I'd know the last to flower would be the best?
It is – or anyway it seems so at this moment –
and although I know that writing about roses
is well out of season, I can't help indulging
for the last time while this last one lasts.

Letting Go

It won't be long before you're ready to strike out
on your own. You'll be in your element
and get a grant, as a mature student
(maybe even land a job when you graduate!).
But back to swimming lessons. Take a breath
and hold it while you dip your head. There! Good!
That's the first step; now you need to learn to float.
Trust me, I'll support you, you won't sink.

Relax while I hold you, give yourself. As if
I'd let you go before you've mastered the knack
of breaking loose from my arms and taking off.
You won't need me, I'd put you off your stroke
unfortunately, but you're learning fast. Good luck.
When I see you off, love, don't look back.

Be missing you

I wish I could miss you while you're still here.
It's like waiting at an airport terminal
for a delayed departure, wanting you gone
so I can settle to remembering your presence.
And then my longings will be more than Faustian.
One minute in your arms will seem enough
to sell the earth for once these numb days
between times are over. You'll come into focus.
Meanwhile I wish you wouldn't sit so close
as I'm shaping the contours of your absence.
Little details like the way your hand on my hand
ought to feel, but doesn't at this moment,
will be felt like cut nerves dangling in space.
'If I could only reach across the miles
and touch your fingertips with mine,' I'll write,
or something like that, after you've left.

Post partum

A difficult labour, though in the end
you seemed to push yourself out
and then I cut the cord with my own teeth.
I dreamt the rest, but don't forget to write
from time to time. The bed I lie in
nightly is the same one we shared
and you wriggled on my belly like a tadpole
with two legs. I loved that – and your beard
all furry and your tongue inside my mouth.

Disappearing Act

Something like an Indian rope-trick but
you were stark naked when you shinned up,
and it was a birch, I think, the way its skin gleamed
smooth and slithery – although it had no branches.
(How quick your thighs were and how strong your sinews.)

It seemed you climbed especially to see me out of sight
whereas, in fact, I was rooted to the spot
and you'd already left by then. (You don't quite
notice an Indian summer's ended till the cloud drops.
At first I couldn't grasp your disappearance into it.)

It's a tricky business like a levitation without props.
I should have had a chance to see you off
and know for sure you'd slid off up that greasy track
into your own life (your quick young thighs, your sinews).
As it is, I'm still uncertain which of us was which.

In Absentia

Apart from you for weeks, I'm dripping with time
to do nothing at all in. I'm rich with space
and abstracts with no contours or context.
After such sheer wealth of shapelessness
who'd ever want to go back into that whole mess
of mixed-up arms and legs – or relive the moment
when my right foot hit the shelf above the bed
and drenched us both in Full Bodied Red?

Old Haunt

Visiting Zennor for the first time since,
I didn't even get out of the car, didn't dare
enter the church and sit where we'd sat
(our veins strung taut as catgut between us).
Someone had carved the mermaid out of longing,
out of absence, you thought (your voice
haunting now in retrospect). I thought
nothing; saw the whiteness of our knuckles; felt
our clasped hands straining, interlocked; heard
some low thrumming in my head like silence.
Was it in the mermaid's ancient wooden face,
worn featureless by time, that you read absence?
We clung so tightly that our hands would never part
but there's a blank already where your face was.

Finds

Remember when we visited Chysauster
and traced the prehistoric water channels
and you remarked on the sophistication
of the ancients? Are you still interested
in antiquities? You ought to view my face
again in close-up. It's sophisticated.
I've found new fosses daily in your absence.

That dig you did (an Iron Age graveyard was it?)
excited me as well. You'd gently opened
the ditch and penetrated till you felt out
soggy bone which would have dissolved on the spot
under a heavy hand. Your touch was so light
but you're young and, as you said, afraid to let
your full weight rest too long in any one place.

Jammed Brakes

Ten hours just to get back here again.
There were so many delays and missed connections
on the way, I had a lot of time to think.
Just before the junction where we were held up
for ages by a freight-train blocking the track
('due to jammed brakes,' the guard announced)
I decided not to visit you again. It was a slog.
But put it down to middle-aged fatigue.

We passed the freight-train, hauled into a siding,
due for decommission I expect. 'Old slag!'
you called me when you finally gave up
and shunted me aside because *you* couldn't make it.
'Apologies for any inconvenience caused.' I'm tired
of jammed brakes, blockage, services disrupted.

On Westminster Bridge

If you were some bimbette and I a man of substance
old enough to be your grandad we could
book a Park Lane penthouse bridal suite
and smooch in public. I would be respected
for my bulging pockets hiding the bare fact
that inflation deflates when my twills come off.

It's sad that I could only seem to be your mum
or some fifty-ish predatory tart. What price
a seedy bed-and-breakfast near Paddington?
Not that either of us could afford it or the risk
of over-exposure to appearances –
snide glances tarnishing the buckled mirrors.

Just walking hand-in-hand seemed bad enough
didn't it? Not that you mentioned what you thought
but it looked better in reflection to link arms instead –
my dear, supportive son and I in Oxford Street
(your right hand coupling with my left in your pocket!).
A real son is more openly affectionate.

At Westminster, though, you assumed your slum-kid look,
slouching apart, and when I paused on the bridge
to look back at the stern, substantial backsides
of government, you said you never noticed contexts,
taking *Boxing News* out of your pocket, on the defensive,
telling me to bugger off and see my son in Cambridge.

Words

Of course our bodies always knew each other
better than our brains did. Nothing's changed.

My eyes have registered your lifted brows
and the way your nostrils twitch in my face.

The whole length of my body up against
your spine learnt that you've grown since we last met.

My feet talked in my sleep. It was a sentence
they remembered like a boot in the teeth.

Between Us

'I hate your guts' rattled down the line
from Cambridge, shuddered to a halt
at Winchmore Hill, which wasn't on my timetable.
You'd said I'd never see you again.

Shrieking your name and stumbling over luggage
and through two doors dividing carriages
to find an exit, I was too late. You'd gone.
The train pulled away from the empty platform.

It could have been the dream I would have dreamt
if I'd slept since I'd last seen you, but I hadn't,
though when I turned and saw your face approaching
those two glass partitions, inside, I didn't think.

How slowly doors slide open then won't shut
due to our bodies. In that interlock
between two carriages we were exposed
and must have entertained the other passengers.

The clinch must have jolted me awake. I think
we're not supposed to do these things in public.
'Fated,' you murmured. 'I love your guts,' I said.
The door you'd entered by was opposite my seat.

I should have noticed it, but my eyes were glazed
with sleeplessness. No trains from Cambridge pass
through Winchmore Hill, we'd both been told
and both believed. The one you missed hadn't.

Sleep-walking at King's Cross, your hand
my anchorage, I dreamt I'd stay another night
in your bed but was too afraid to wake up
too late or too soon to catch the ghost between us.

A Change in the Weather, Underground

Side by side, backs to the window,
counting stations back down the Northern Line,
we had nothing at all to talk about. Why should we?
At Tottenham Court Road we said 'Goodbye'
and brushed lips briefly, decently, as if
I could have been your aunt, say? The doors opened, closed.

There was that one last glance over your shoulder
as the train pulled out. I'd call it speechless.
Meanwhile, I couldn't understand. I watched my feet
following the blurred signs to the Central Line
and they walked me through the gusty passageways
as if they knew directions, though I didn't.

At Paddington I saw two such as us meeting
as we'd met three days before, trembling, searching
each other's faces for answers, questions.
Like us they headed for the Underground
hand-in-hand, and I remembered what you'd said
about the weather down there, all those crosswinds.

Last Remains

It was you who lit the fire and started
feeding my letters into it out of
the stuffed dustbin-liner, like a body-bag.
I assisted. The cremation was not too sad.
But who'd have thought there would be such a wad
of ashes left to cover with a boulder and commit to earth?
'Dust to dust,' you think, washing your hands of it,
feeling almost glad. That's one life less to cope with.

The wind must have been strong last night. Dead leaves
are all over the garden, black-edged, crinkled,
and, amongst them, others, slightly paler than the rest.
Surprised by words and half-words like hieroglyphs,
I gathered up 'alway', 'orever', 'love';
couldn't capture something that might have been 'PS'.

Last Year in Dorset

Oh I can see you, I can just imagine you
with her and hear you saying it's the first time
and forever always was, and sweating. I can
feel and smell you all wet and you're coming...

Scenic interlude on Chesil Beach,
pebbles in close-up; your eyes hooded.
Is the tide coming in or going out?

'It's never ever happened like this before,'
you're saying. Liar! And I bet you lie with her
inside her afterwards as if you can't bear
to withdraw. I bet you care. I bet you haven't
yet got out and up and zipped yourself into your jeans
as quickly as you did that last night in Bridport
when I didn't say so but could tell it was all over
and your irritation when we tried once more
and you got nowhere and I want you so much
that I hope you meet a sudden death inside her.

The Proposition

Looked you straight in the eyes and said she felt
like reproducing? Were you flattered? I'm glad
you said you didn't want to be a daddy yet.
But I've never tried to own you and still don't.

'No ties, no obligations.' Did that turn you on?
O brave new world of sex without a condom!
Was her blood-donor badge in evidence?
But I've never tried to own you and still don't.

Just don't forget that I'm the only woman
you risk nothing with, not even a child
('enough of *us* already!' you once joked).
But I've never tried to own you and still don't.

Washing Instructions

When you wear the sweater I bought for you
especially because you like black and I knew
the style would suit you, think of me.
I chose lambswool for your warmth and comfort
but you look far too good in it for safety.
Even before the train pulled out
that girl who plonked herself opposite your seat
was making sheep's eyes at you I noticed.
Thanks for the note asking how to care for it.
Best thing would be to dunk it in a sheep-dip.
Failing that, boil for thirty minutes
then wring hard and stuff it in an oven
to dry out. (Set at top heat for quick results.)
Good of you to spare the time to ask for my advice.

'For Refund, Insert Baby Here'

A monster love-child, born out of season.
Please don't think I ever wanted this
misshapen creature suckling at my head
and wailing through my mouth to be cherished,
but I'm stuck with it since all precautions failed.
You should have killed the miserable brat at birth.

So I couldn't even laugh at that joke
some bloke had scratched on a condom-dispenser
in the Gents. (I get suspicious when you mention
condoms now in any context, and your brief note
didn't say much else, did it? You forgot
even to send your love this time for instance.)
If I'd still been young enough to bear your real child
I never would have whelped this snivelling runt.

Writing for Two

Today I made up words for you to write
in your hand. (I've assimilated it.)
Your letter throbbed with longing, said
you couldn't eat, sleep, work or anything
without me, said you'd give the world if
we could only start again from scratch.

I sealed the envelope, addressed it to myself
marked URGENT, stamped it, ran to catch the post.
Tomorrow I shall have a reason to get up.
My heart's already thudding at the thought
of one white envelope addressed in your hand
lying on the mat. Maybe I'll pick it up,
chuck it in the bin, shan't read it. You get fed up,
sending junk mail back marked 'Unsolicited'.

Cold Shower

Okay, we'd drunk too much. A good excuse
for you to nearly bite my tongue off? It bled.
'Maybe that will stop your mouth,' you muttered.
(The night before you'd said I must be deaf.)
So when you got a glassful of cold water
in your face, I think you'd finally deserved it.

Getting your things together, getting dressed,
asking what I'd done with your towel, your socks,
double-knotting the laces of your trainers,
'Good riddance to bad rubbish!' I hissed.
At 3 a.m. precisely, the door slammed shut.
This time I was certain you would not come back,
but when I found you huddled on the doorstep,
frozen, you were glad of my hot blood.

Cross Words

Your silence when we're having words is deep.
I'd rather chuck encyclopaedias about
than listen to the crackle of your static.
Just how many times must I repeat
that we need to get acquainted again *first*,
before we go to bed? You only come back here for sex.
'It's like fucking a dictionary,' you said,
and that was that. I'd only wanted to communicate.

But you complete the crossword in five minutes flat
while I'm pondering one clue under the surface.
Once you groaned that no one makes a crossword
hard enough for you to have to puzzle over for a bit.
Such cleverness! Such failure to plunge deep enough
into your own heart, even! 'Stingray', I came up with.

Happy Ever After

The times they are a-changing-O,
a-changing-O, a-changing now
that *happy ever after* means *tomorrow,
fingers crossed.* The fairy tales grow
grimmer as the spent fuel rods mount up.
Rapunzel combs her locks and they fall out
in tufts. Beauty's dress is salmonella-pink.
Listeria creeps into the final feast
up at the palace where the trees have rotted
and Aurora and her retinue drop dead
for keeps. The prince proves positive
at birth and fades away into the sunset
of his royal blood before he's even kissed yet.

The times they are a-changing-O,
a-changing-O, a-changing now
that *happy ever after* means *tomorrow,
fingers crossed.* The fairy tales grow
grimmer as the ozone layer breaks up.
So yes, let's build our bivouac and camp
together here forever. What's an age gap
of some twenty years? We still have teeth,
eyes, ears, hair, flesh, and lips to kiss with.
The wicked witch has come into her own at last?
She always wept in cackles. What a laugh!
Look! We have come through! (so far, at least)
warmer by the minute as the permafrost melts.

Explication de Texte

To summarise what might have been the plot:
'Young man loves, then casts off, older woman.'
Usual theme: 'Impossible relationship'.
Wouldn't that be neat? And after all we part
so regularly and it's always a relief
for a day or two, before we reunite.
We seem to spend more time on station platforms
than in bed, although the trains are rarely late.

And so, to start again, let's reinterpret:
what if he doesn't give a fig about her age
or his, but she is haunted by a past
in which such fine distinctions counted?
Consider how she triggers words – Russian roulette?
Playing recklessly with time before time snuffs it?

Something Like a Wedding?

Not much of a sale for that jeweller
with the blue-rinse, but she didn't turn a hair.
On Saturdays she's Priestess of the Ring Counter,
treating each odd match as a solemn affair
as if she were a vicar or a registrar.
It felt a bit like standing at an altar.

No promises for better or for worse, of course –
just a ritual of trying rings for size
(me wishing my hand looked as young as yours).
'Will you wear them now or shall I put them in a box?'
'A box,' I said, as if they were for corpses.
She was already sizing up the two behind us.

Those gale-force winds hustling us through town
weren't ceremonious, and neither were we solemn
when we each slipped our own thin silver ring on.
Our Priestess had said we'd got an end-of-line bargain.
Dust's our confetti in this mixed-up season.
'Even love won't part us,' I vowed up through the ozone.

The Ring and Gobbledegook

But for the ring, nothing would have happened
before I lost it. Take, for instance,
that you never would have wished to strangle me
or cut my head off if I hadn't tried
to talk you out of it? (I used to like
the Gobbledegook you spoke to me in sleep
and was learning to translate the language backwards.)
My ring disappeared overnight after that.

A thin white noose of skin is all that's left,
like a reminder. I'm fixated on this nakedness.
My finger's vulnerable as a corpse and I'm bereft,
but that's the reason why you can't come back,
which is why you drank the last dregs of your grant
and ended the beginning, if I've got the sequence right.

'Home'

How many bruises you've inflicted on me
since the first one I can't count. But *again*
you're desperate and must come 'home'. It's urgent.
Okay then, you can have the bed we shared
once like true lovers. I'll feel safer in my own.
I lie in it as in a narrow tomb
but at least you've failed to kick my door in yet.

Please try not to smash the house up this time
as you did in April, and I dumped you at the station
yet *again*, with such relief, O Brave New Man!
I can't afford another rail-fare. You should hitch
like other students – those fortunate enough
to have homes to go back to. You've slept rough
on benches, but sleep rougher here in bed.

Well, I know you have no family to help you out
or put you up, and student dole's been cut,
and even if you tried you wouldn't find a summer job.
So what choice do I have except to let you back
again – and pay for it? I can't afford
to have the unhinged doors fixed. 'Home' looks a mess,
as if it's carved-up ready to be repossessed.

'Domestic'

'We see dozens of domestics every week,'
one of the cops said, reassuringly.
Seems I was lucky that I hadn't snuffed it
totally – just throttled and my head and face bashed up.
Oh, we were growing more domestic by the minute
since grants and housing-benefit were cut
and my lover had nowhere else but here to live
so he said I had to die 'because of poll tax'.

'Is this man your son?' they'd asked.
Final irony. Pity I couldn't laugh.
He used to joke: 'If anybody ever asks you that,
say I'm your dad.' I saw him out in handcuffs.
If it's true that each man kills the thing he loves
it was himself he really meant to finish off.

£50 Compensation

For what? For loss of life or just
to help towards the cost of laying-out
and stitching up the corpse to make it look
quite lifelike, really, considering?
Maybe it's compensation for shrinkage?
(How come the soul has such an airy weightlessness
that it plumps out the body prior to death?)
Cover all mirrors, just in case.

Justice has been seen to have been done
and fifty quid must be the going-rate
this year for changing a face into a death-mask.
Why should 'bodily harm' eat out the spirit?
'We each give as good as we get,' he told me once,
but only one of us gave, and paid the price.

ALSO FROM BLOODAXE BOOKS

Dirty Washing
NEW & SELECTED POEMS
SYLVIA KANTARIS

'Her work is powerful, sensual, passionate and controlled. She avoids paltry sentimentality, and is viciously ironic when it suits her subject-matter...A poet of considerable skill' – BRITISH BOOK NEWS

The words most often used to describe Sylvia Kantaris's poetry are *passionate* and *powerful*. Her poems are cutting and touching, funny and furious, and – above all – vital. She isn't afraid to speak from the heart, to take risks. The wide range of her work combines with her intensely daring approach to blow the cobwebs from some well-worn poetic territory and light up some of the dark corners of life and love. *Dirty Washing* includes a very generous helping of new poems, and draws on four earlier books: *Time & Motion* (1975), *The Tenth Muse* (1983), *The Sea at the Door* (1985), and her collaboration with D.M. Thomas, *News from the Front* (1983).

'Kantaris writes clearly, frankly, movingly and humorously about a wide variety of human relationships' – PETER READING, *Sunday Times*

'There's a brash and sexy note in many of the poems...It's a finely judged selection, and makes for continually engrossing reading' – PETER FORBES, *The Listener*

'The new poems in *Dirty Washing* confirm Kantaris not only as sensitive lyricist but also as a speaker of painful truths, as a satirist, and as a poet who can fuse the colloquial and the elegiac, the factual and the surrealist, in single poems of deceptive simplicity' – JAMES AITCHISON, *Glasgow Herald*

'She is a poet so full of energy and dash that her poetry brims over with a kind of expectation of good weather...Her language is wonderfully sensual and in her exchange with D.M. Thomas we can see the contrast between his crabbed aversion to sex and her attraction, despite the swapping of roles and gender between them...Excesses are necessary to her style' – S.J. LITHERLAND, *The Green Book*

ALSO FROM BLOODAXE BOOKS

The Air Mines of Mistila
POETRY BOOK SOCIETY CHOICE
SYLVIA KANTARIS & PHILIP GROSS

High above the plain, beyond the village of Hum, up where the mountainside melts into cloud, lies an unmapped plateau. Here people appear out of thin air. And disappear. Or so they say. *Mistila...*

Sylvia Kantaris and Philip Gross have been there. Or so they claim. Her son was in Colombia, and he told her about this place, Mistila, in an air-letter. She mentioned it to Philip Gross.

All poets steal. Gross was no exception. Almost by return post, he sent her a poem. She replied. In three months they populated the Mistilan plateau with a cast of characters who live, eke out their livelihoods, and die. Like us. Almost.

In the strange atmospheric conditions of Mistila, you may glimpse Cornish mineshafts to a background of Andean condor music. You may feel vertigo, hilarity or grief, see mirages of the real world and its threats. If you return, you'll wonder what is true, in this place conjured out of air.

'*The Air Mines of Mistila* is a Poetry Book Society Choice, and one can readily see why. Quirky and riddling and fleet of foot, it is the happy collaboration between two poets who have conjured up a fantasy from a shared stimulus' – DAVID PROFUMO, *Sunday Times*

'An engaging fancy and one which is inventively carried through by the two poets involved. They've created a society which exists somewhere in an imaginary South America and this allows for a range of satiric commentary on societies a good deal nearer home... Well worth buying' – JOHN LUCAS, *New Statesman*

'Philip Gross and Sylvia Kantaris combine their considerable gifts to create a colourful peopled world, lit up by "magic realism"'
– JOHN KERRIGAN, *London Review of Books*

'Valuable, very funny and wildly imaginative' – GLYN MAXWELL, *Poetry Review*

Sylvia Kantaris was born in 1936 in the Derbyshire Peak District. She studied French at Bristol University, taught in Bristol and London, and then spent ten years in Australia, where she taught French at Queensland University, had two children, and wrote her MA and PhD theses on French Surrealism.

In 1974 she settled in Cornwall, at Helston, and from 1976 to 1984 tutored 20th Century Poetry for the Open University. In 1986 she was appointed Cornwall's first Writer in the Community, and in 1989 received an honorary D.Litt from Exeter University.

Her first two books of poems, *Time & Motion* (Prism/Poetry Society of Australia, 1975) and *The Tenth Muse* (Peterloo Poets, 1983), were both reissued by Menhir Press in 1986. Her third collection, *The Sea at the Door* (Secker & Warburg, 1985), is no longer available.

She has published two joint collections with other poets, *News from the Front* with D.M. Thomas (Arc, 1983), and *The Air Mines of Mistila* with Philip Gross (Bloodaxe Books, 1988), a Poetry Book Society Choice.

Her latest titles are *Dirty Washing: new & selected poems* (Bloodaxe Books, 1989), including work from all her previous books except *The Air Mines of Mistila*, and a new collection, *Lad's Love* (Bloodaxe Books, 1993).